Amidst Fading Blooms
POEMS

REGINA BERGEN

To myself...
... and my heart.

Someday, everything will work out just as it was meant to be.

The Truth About Flowers

Flowers don't ask for permission to grow.
They burst, unapologetically, through the dirt,
Rising from the tiniest seed—a mere speck—
To become nature's brightest firework display.

Ask a sunflower why it's pushed upward to the sky,
And thrown its petals proudly towards the sun.
It will tell you that's just what it was born to do.
Ask a rose why it's shoved thorns from its stems,
And you will find it's been hurt before; it needed protection.

Each bloom, each stem, each thorn, each blossom
Tells a story all its own—but never is there an apology.
Never is there a sorrowful refusal to go on living.
They rise, they bloom, they fade, and they fall,
Seeding the Earth with the next life cycle.

Flowers grow because they were meant to.
We, too, should do the same—survive and thrive.
Never ask for permission to do as we're supposed—

To bloom where we are planted or catch the wind and fly.

Never apologize for having our thorns out if it keeps us safe.
Flower freely and embrace the storms as they come,
Weathering them as best we can and bending with the wind.
Stay standing through the hard times, pivot as needed,
But always bounce back, stand tall, and show our true colors.

Flowers don't ask for permission to grow, nor should we.

Mother

Storm clouds float in, ready to burst,
Dark and thick with midnight rain.
They guard their contents, refusing to release
Showers that threaten to pour eternally.
Once they start, it's hard to stop.

I, too, hold in tears that yearn to be shed.
Salty streams that I've bottled up deep inside,
Clinging to them since the day you left this world.
My heart aches for you like the stormy skies crave the sun.
I long to see you just one more time.

If just to say the things I never said but you always knew.
You used to light up my sky on the darkest of days.
You were my sunshine—my only sunshine.
Each moment that passes now, I think of you.
Even more than the ones before.

You've touched every part of my life
And made me who I am today through lessons

That ring in my ears, even long after your passing.

Now, I feel you in the breeze.
I see you in the clouds.
I hear you in the songs of the birds.

You are all around me, preaching lessons of:
Love
Forgiveness
Hope
Compassion
Understanding
Perseverance
Kindness
And of pure, unadulterated strength.

You were a warrior.
You are—and always will be—my mother.

Weeping Willow

I see you there, weeping willow,
With sadness in your stare,
Limbs bent under the weight of your sorrow.
Don't let it own you, though.
Your branches may be bent,
But they are not broken.
You can weather the storm like no other,
Flexible and strong. Mighty.
Embrace the lessons you've learned
Along the way, and become a powerful force
To be reckoned with for any wrongdoers
Who should attempt to bring you harm.
Weep, willow, as you were meant to weep—
Bend, willow, as you were meant to bend—
And never let them see you cry.

The Guardian

You stand tall, sheltering others from the storm,
Reeking of petrichor as you fold your arms against
The mighty sting of the cold, ancient rains.
You are their guardian, their protector.
For, you've always had to be the one.
But who will rise up to save you from the
Relentlessly pelting drops of chaos you endure?
You can be their guiding starlight for only so long,
Before you become lost within yourself.
The sun's rays can no longer penetrate your darkness,
Once you've clung to it for too long.
Let it go, let it be, let it ride, let it free.
For just one time, let them be their own saviors.
Allow yourself to be the protected rather than the protector.
Stand beneath the cover of the branches of the others,
And tell them you need—you deserve—a break.
You can't meet their needs when you're falling apart.

First Snow

Bright sun streams from above,
Throwing glitter into the air.
And for the first time in years,
Winter's first snow feels like magic.

Finally, a reprieve from the pain,
A break from mundane sorrow.
The icy air chills the body,
But warms the soul with festive joy.

As the sky sends its shimmering gifts down,
They fall like a shower of hope for things to come.
For once, there may be a better tomorrow—
A promise that dreams can still come true.

Finally, the ever-so-slight possibility that all isn't lost.

Searching

She drives for hours
with the windows down
in the pouring rain—
Captures its intoxicating scent
and breathes it in like a drug.
She'll do anything to remember
that she is still of this Earth—
and carries part of its magic in her veins.
But now, the magic has lost its luster.
It's dull and lifeless, like herself as of late.
So, she searches for sparks in her past,
amidst the nearly-forgotten memories
of the people and places long ago left behind.
She presses on with each moment, each day—
barely making it through the endless nights,
hoping to ignite her future with a sparkle
that she used to know so very well.
Desperately seeking to rekindle the flames
once felt so strongly in her every move,
she reaches out for anything within reach—

A lingering heat that burns like embers,
carrying the promise, or even just the hope,
Of white-hot flame if tended with her very being.
If she gives it all that she is, all that she has,
Will it become a fire that will withstand the pouring rain,
and shimmer with the promise of possibilities?

She Cries

She cries in the night, but there's no one there to hear.
It's nothing more than a breath on the wind—
Silent and solitary.
Her tears are set against a raging river—
Unnoticeable, indistinguishable.
The rushing waters fill her sea and keep her skies
shrouded in darkness.
She cries at night, but would the sun's light
make any difference?

Stolen

Here lies stolen purity,
offered up in hopes that
she'd be something to someone.
It didn't happen quickly.
Traded sanctity slowly
over many lonely nights.
She lost herself.
Found herself.
Then, gave it all away.
Now, the tears come in waves,
intermingled with numbness—
And the occasional intrusion
of unadulterated rage.
She faded like a flower
left thirsty for too long.
Feasted on poison.
Drugged herself to feel again,
Hungering for the smallest hint
of the promise of tomorrow.

Now, each one means less
than the one from the night before—
And she's too broken to be just an option
but too frightened to be more.

Fear

She had been a subtle glimmer
Of the girl she was before,
Until his lips pressed against hers,
Pulling her into his world.
The light became magnified;
The darkness somehow brightened—
And everything was as it should be,
But she couldn't accept it as real.
The electricity of his touch was pure heat,
Igniting her inner passions,
Illuminating her eyes
And setting a fire between her thighs.
But fear took over,
Its long fingers reaching in with a death grip,
Ripping it to shreds—
All that could have been.

Enough

No longer will I let my heart be owned
By those who seek to destroy it—
To watch as it melts away in the flames
Of their words or lack thereof.

Enough.

No longer will I be the weak one,
The empty, the needy—
The one who always waits.

Enough.

No longer will I cling to every sentence,
Hoping for just one more word,
Or a lingering stare to comfort, to calm.

Enough.

No longer will I cling to your texts.

Every. Single. Message.
The ones you give so sparingly.

Enough!

I'm worth more than this, I know.
But my heart is still frail from trauma,
And seeks love in all the wrong places.

It runs away when something real
Threatens to pierce its thick skin,
And pose the risk of any true loss.

So, instead, I cling to the little you give,
Hoping that someday it will be enough.
Forgetting that I'm already enough.

Enough.

Without you,
I am enough.

Still

Your words—so soft, so sweet,
Yet, lethal pinpricks to my heart.

You give them out freely,
Then, rip them away.

Each time your tongue moves,
I start to come unglued.

I know I'm not the only one.
Still, I cling to your carefully curated words.

They escape your mouth like poetry.
But I know someone else hears them, too.

Still, I answer when you call.
Still, I come running if you ask.

I want what will never be.
I yearn for someone you're not.

And the worst part is, I know it.
I've always known it.
Yet, I'm still here waiting, hoping.

Will I ever escape this tug-of-war?
This endless back and forth?

Will I find something else to replace
the longing to fill the void within you?
Or the one inside of me?

Or will I stand by as you push me down,
Again and again, until I'm flat on the dirt?

Unable to move,
Unable to breathe,
Unable to live.

Will I let you wear me down into nothing,
And watch me fade away?

I will because I keep coming back for more.
I just keep coming back.

Where the Air is Thin

When he's not with me,
The air seems too thin.
Like it's somehow not enough
To keep me alive.

It leaves me stranded,
Gasping for breath.
Yearning for a call—
Or some small bit of attention.

Anything to fight the numbness,
And the excruciating pain of knowing
That I will never be enough for him.
I'm simply not enough.

Mistakes

How do you tabulate all the mistakes you've made in a year?
Do you count them in one-night stands?
In the number of times you've been ghosted?
Or how often you've ghosted someone else?

After a while, even the successes start to feel like failures.

He was great, but it didn't last.
He was sweet, but I got scared and ran away.
I liked him. Turns out, I was his side chick—
And his wife found out.
I could have loved him, but he was as
Emotionally unavailable as I am damaged.
He was fun while it lasted, but apparently,
That's all this ever was.
I would have picked him,
But he told me we were just friends.

Those benefits, though.
That's where they get you.

How many mistakes does it take
Before you start to respect yourself?
How many errors in judgment?
Attention-seeking errors?
How many times before you start to realize
It's not worth it?

At some point, it's just not worth it.
It's not enough.
You're worth more than any of this.

Sooner or later, I'll see it... Won't I?

Lovesick

It comes through like a whirlwind—a wolf in sheep's clothing.
That sickness, that disease, that... LOVE.
It traps you, leaving you weak, frail, and blind—
Unable to escape or retrace your steps,
The movements that led you to this place of poison.
All the while, you thought it was what you wanted.
All along, it was what you'd been searching for.
All that time wasted seeking nothing more than a sickness.
How could you have been so wrong, so misinformed?
This love is nothing short of insanity—
An unhinged,
Agonizing,
Attachment.
An emptiness that leaves you gasping for air,
Clinging to the chaos because it's better than being alone.
They don't call it lovesick for nothing, you know.

Burn

At the crossroads of love or hate—
Give or take—
Stay or leave—
You chose to walk out the door—
And for that, I hope you burn.

Living Nightmare

Sometimes, the dullness seeps in, and there's no escaping
The crushing mental blow dealt by
One too many nights spent alone,
Pouring over thoughts of what was,
—What could be, what should be—
But what will, assuredly, never become your reality.
Numbness seeps in through skin-deep cuts,
Oozing beneath your skin and into your inner being,
Until it takes over all that you are—and becomes you.
Never asking permission and never saying sorry,
You become one with the feeling of nothingness.
Yet, still, you receive no apologies for the blunting
That takes everything and offers absolutely nothing in return.
Sometimes, you let the lack of emotion clench its fists,
And overtake you entirely because the alternative is terrifying.
Should the nothingness disappear,
You'll have to feel everything else—
And that's a waking nightmare of epic proportions.

Alone

Anger comes at the worst possible moment,
Leaving me void of words, throat dry, feeling vindictive.
But the rage quickly transforms into tears.
Instead, I appear small, weak, and pathetic—
Everything I never want you to see in me.
What's worse than being with you?
Being alone and broken with you watching.

Who Am I?

I am...
Independent—because I'm alone.
Strong—because there's no room left for weakness.
Fearless—because I have nothing left to lose.
Unique—because no one else has faced my trauma.
Capable—because if I didn't do it, who would?
Outspoken—because there's no one else to speak for me.
Creative—because I would have failed long ago, otherwise.
Committed—because the alternative is broke or homeless.
Courageous—because there are no other options.
A Dreamer—because I can't afford to
Let the nightmares take over.
I am all these things and more—
Just a blossom struggling to survive
Amidst fading blooms.

What You Give

All the things you offer me ebb and flow like the tide.
With you, there's no such thing as in-between.
It's all or nothing—but it's never all the time.
You float my heart up to the sky and into the clouds.
You raise it up on a bed of false hope.
Your beautiful words weave a net, so I feel secure—
But there are never any promises spoken, only implied.
It feels like you give me your everything,
But I know tomorrow we will return to nothing.
Still, it's enough to keep me coming back.
Your ties aren't merely chains but barbed wire.
Roses with thorny branches disguised as loving hands.
You pull the tethers tighter each time I'm about to escape—
And pierce the skin with flesh wounds that feel much deeper.
So, I stay behind waiting for the day you give me everything,
Only to cut it off once again and leave me begging for more.

Storm Clouds

The wind kicks up as branches whip angrily,
In anticipation of the oncoming deluge.
A distant rumbling fills the skies,
Vibrating the ground below,
And forcing my dogs into hiding.

I wish I could hide from it all so easily.

We once felt safe in the confines of these walls,
Those safeguards that protected us from loneliness.
Now, they are no more than prison bars,
Keeping us locked in by past decisions
And piss-poor judgment.
Now, we've learned to anticipate a storm at least daily.

And when it rains, it pours—violent words, fists into walls.

Our past sins and transgressions flow like flooded rivers,
Pouring out in words of rage and hatred—like venom.
We used to sip champagne in the light of the moon,

Stars filling the sky, fireflies flickering like glitter.
It was magic ignited by the power and promise of possibility.

But now that's all dead and gone.

You invited those killjoy storms in with open arms,
Welcomed them into the safety and sanctity of our home—
And let them invade our space like an enemy army.

You chose betrayal over the prospect of our future.
... And all because I was never enough.

I would never have been enough.

Waves

These waves of sorrow pull me out,
Deeper into a sea of despair.
Their power ebbs and flows like the tide,
But never fades entirely, never releases their grasp.
They are an ever-present reminder of where I've been—
And that I still don't know where I'm going.
Always there, rushing in, then me pulling back,
Weathering away the remaining layers of my heart—
Until it feels like there isn't much left to save.
My arms rise in pathetic attempts to tread water,
And protect the little that's still worth shielding
From the crushing weight of the waves,
From the inevitable drowning and fading into the abyss,
With the always-triggering memory of his words.

Yours

Raindrops swell heavy and wide just before they break,
Sending them tumbling down the windowpane in streams—
Like tears shed late at night under cover of darkness,
After you shattered my hopes one too many times.
You held my heart in your hands, drunk with that power.
You relished the knowledge that it was glass,
And you were its keeper, to have, or to hold,
To care for, or to crush—the choice was yours,
Yours and yours alone, and you loved every last moment
Of knowing you were my prison guard and grim reaper.

Self-Sabotage

I ran away from love again and chose the wrong one instead.
Self-sabotage in the name of self-preservation.
It's my specialty, after all, don't you know?
Stupidity at its finest, but I do it again and again.
I let him go free; too tied up in my own protection—
Afraid to love after the crash and burn of the time before.
It happened slowly at first this time—
Like fog settling over a vast expanse.
The regret seeped in and took over,
Uncertainty arriving piece by piece,
Until it was all-encompassing—
And it was far too late to make amends.
Then it came on fast and strong,
The longing and wishful thinking.
Hoping against hope that there would be another chance,
An opportunity to make things right—
To fix those things that can't ever be fixed,
All the while knowing that his ship had already sailed.
Play stupid games, win stupid prizes—

And wind up alone,
Praying that someday you'll get it right.

Paper Heart

You took your scissored hands and made
Slices through my paper heart,
Under the false pretense that you were merely
Decorating it for our love story.
I took it into my hands and ran, arriving home to find,
Upon unfolding it,
Only the snowflake of remnants you left behind
—ice cold and frozen—
Far beyond the possibility of repair,
Never to feel warmth ever again.
Now an ice queen, I've abandoned all thoughts
Of seeking love again.
You created this monster—and a monster I shall remain.
I can slay my own dragons now.
I can dig my own grave.

Shards

My mind feels like the sky when it's been sunless for too long.
Cloudy, foggy, dull—the light too easily lost to the darkness.
My heart feels like the basement of an abandoned house.
Musty emptiness seeps into the spaces where it's cracked,
Freezing it in an icy embrace until it
Shatters into lethal shards,
Much too sharp to pick up and put back together.

Starting Over

You're here even when you're gone,
A lingering darkness I once thought was my light.
You're a distant memory in my waking moments,
But you still haunt my dreams, vivid and terrifying.
You're a force that bled the life from me,
Laughing as you walked away and left me in the dust
To start over, no longer a believer in happy endings,
And burdened with the heaviness of the past.

Damaged

What right did you have to attach yourself to my heart,
Knowing deep down that you didn't want mine in return?
Now that it's all over, does goodbye hurt you even a little?
Can you feel an ounce of the pain that comes
With what-might-have-been?
You could have been my everything,
But chose to be my nothing-at-all.
It hurts, but I know that I'll heal—
But you won't ever be whole.
You're too far gone for that now,
Lost in the despair of your numbness.

Fallen

I used to think I'd make something of myself.
Have a beautiful life.
Become something great.
Earn respect.
Make a difference.
Matter.
I was always good at so many things.
Fast learner.
Smart.
Driven.
Must have driven until I got lost.
I'm not exactly sure where I let the ball drop.
Here I am, though.
Just look at me now.
Alone.
Imposter syndrome.
Loveless.
Friendless.
Fading fast.
Awaiting my redemption.

Love Language

The only love language you know is deception.
It's in your gaze, your touch, your words.
You bleed lies from cuts on your venomous tongue,
And somehow, I still believe every last one.
I welcomed your promises with open arms,
Trusting in your heart completely for too long.
For mine didn't yet know how to sow destruction.
Don't worry, though. I'm a fast learner.
I took your smiles as true and your touches as tender.
Who was I to think anything less of you?
Young and dumb, my love language was attention,
And you piled it on thick, until the day you stopped.

Foreward

No one ever asked me what I wanted from life.
It simply was, simply is, simply will be.
Life doesn't take requests or dedications.
It's a game, and it's rigged to the house.

You can spout out pretty words about hopes,
Dreams, and manifesting your destiny all day.
But in the end, it's not you who decides.
You're either ahead, behind, or stagnant.

All you can do is try to keep moving forward.
When life gets hard,
Keep moving forward.
When things seem impossible,
Keep moving forward.
When the world chews you up and spits you out,
Keep moving forward.
When you feel like a hamster stuck in a wheel,
Keep moving forward.

Life isn't going to take it easy on you.
All you can do is put one foot in front of the other—
And keep moving forward.
None of us will make it out of life alive, anyway.

Crush

You came to me with branches so strong,
And I crushed them with my heaviness—
My heart, laden with shrapnel.
My mind, riddled with anxiety.
My trauma, a burden you weren't meant to bear.
I piled it on, bending your limbs until
You couldn't withstand the weight of my sorrow.
It snapped your branches, each buckling under the pressure.
I watched from the sidelines as it brought you down,
Unable to protect you from the inevitable fall—
But look at it this way…
No one was there to protect me, either.

Nothing

What we are,
What we were,
What we will be—
All the same answer.
Nothing.
Never was.
Never will be.
But I've given too much of myself
To come out of this empty-handed.
So, I just keep pretending we
Are more than we are—so much more.
It takes two to build something
From the ground up, piece by piece—
But we never made it past the basement.
That's where my bedroom is, after all.

Parachute

Don't let yourself fall in love,
If you don't know how
To stop yourself in mid-air…
It's only the landing that hurts.
Bring a parachute. And a spare.

Ambivalence

I don't know how to tell you how I feel,
So, I'll keep it stored away, carefully concealed,
Until the day you feel the same or...
I'll take it to my death, a burden I'll carry gladly,
Rather than face your ambivalence toward me—
A fate infinitely worse than a lifetime of silence.

Float

Choppy seas kick up inside my heart.
A storm is brewing beneath the surface.
As the currents grow stronger,
These tides pull away from your gravity.
No longer will I let you lasso me in with words.
It's stupid that I thought this could be real,
I was a plaything—and you grew bored.
Sometimes the mistakes hurt just as much,
If not more, than the best of intentions.
So, I let myself float far away on your sea of insincerity.

Boys

Don't.
Let.
Me.
Fall.
Into.
Feelings.
For.
Another.
Boy.
Pretending.
To.
Be.
A.
Man.

Sinking

You're not who I thought you were.
As time goes by your uniqueness fades.
As it turns out, you're just like all the others.
Not sure how you fooled me so fully, though.
You left me clinging to every single word,
As it escaped your still-perfectly formed mouth.
I sidelined plans and prospects out of false hope
For something I knew deep down wouldn't happen.
And the stupidity of it all still stings.
Who are you to turn me clingy and weak,
Leaving me lonely, waiting for a grain of affection?
Who are you to make me feel like I needed
Anyone else beyond myself to feel complete?
No one. You're no one, but, still, I fell for your act,
Hook, line, and sinker—and now I'm sinking.

How?

How do you keep someone who doesn't want to be kept?
It's simple. You don't. You can't. You won't.
And if you try, you'll surely regret the attempt,
You'll crash and burn. Sink and drown.
Accept your certain, unavoidable demise.
You can't love someone who runs from it,
And expect to be loved in return. You won't be.
It's merely fleeting lust that loses its glimmer,
And you'll be left alone to sift through the wreckage.
You can't change him. You won't. He's too far gone—
And, in simple terms, he's just not that into you.

Erased

If I could, I'd rewrite our history to erase the magical nights
That led me to believe that we could become more than
Mere heavy breathing, skin on skin, and lusty words.
I'd give it all back just for a chance to get you
Off my mind, now that I know the ending.
Maybe someday I'll get my fairytale,
But this sure as shit was not it.
This was a nightmare.
You and me.
The End.
Ouch.

Stood Up

I waited for you to call again last night,
After I promised I wouldn't do it again.
Surprise, surprise—you didn't.
I don't know how many times
I will fall for your lies.
Whether intentional or not,
They should have long ago
Proved that I'm merely an option
Who has made you her priority
Time and time again, like clockwork.
For someone who is supposed to be smart,
I sure do act dumb, right?
You don't have to answer—
I already know the truth.

White Flag

I can't breathe.
The air seems thin.
Sucking.
Choking.
Squeezing.
Clenching.
Anxiety forces the air from my lungs,
Never allowing it to be replaced.
I can't do this anymore.
I can't live like this.
I can't breathe.
How do I catch up?
Where do I start?
What do I do?
There's no help to be had.
I'm crippled, unable to move.
Bound to the mess I've made.
It feels crushing—the responsibilities.
Be the perfect mom.

Be a good maid.
Be a gourmet chef.
Be a dedicated writer.
Be an effective editor.
Hit those deadlines.
Meet those goals.
Live your dreams.
You know what?
Fuck my dreams!
I don't even know what they are.
And—I don't even fucking care.
I just want to go to sleep,
Let the silence wash over me.
I beg it to come relieve the stress,
To remove some of the pressure.
Something has got to give.
I can't breathe anymore.
There are too many balls in the air,
And this juggler is losing her focus.
I have lost my kindness in the chaos.
I feel trapped by the have-to's,
Abandoned by the want-to's.
And my heart yearns for something.
Something beyond the daily hustle,
Necessary to merely stay afloat.
Afloat, but never ever ahead.
I'm drowning anyway, so why not sink?
Sometimes I just want to dive down,
And see where I wind up if I just stop trying.
No more treading water to keep up with it all.
Just stop putting forth the effort.
Let it all go—give it up—just be—just exist.
I never asked for any of this, anyway.

AMIDST FADING BLOOMS

I just want to be able to breathe again.
My world is cluttered and chaotic—
And my heart feels the same.
There has to be something beyond
This dull, numb ache that I face each day.
There must be a place of oxygen.
Freedom.
Options.
Real dreams.
A place where I can be myself.
Unjudged.
Unhindered.
Uncaged.
An escape from the everyday fakeness.
A place where, sometimes, being weak is okay—
And breathing isn't an Olympic sport.
I crave the ability to function... or not,
Without worrying about catastrophic repercussions
Life divvies out luck with such reckless abandon.
I certainly never asked to do all of this alone.
The goals now are to wake up and just keep breathing—
Even when there's no air to be had.
Even when the world spins out of control.
Even when life seems less than worthy of living.
Even when you're expected to be everything
To everyone, and get nothing in return.
Even when the clock stops dead in its tracks,
And the minutes feel like days.
Wake up, breathe, keep breathing—
Sometimes, I just don't want to.
It's too much to take, too much to carry.
Heavy.
Burdensome.

Life feels like a brick dragging me down,
And I don't have the will to fight it.
So, I let it take me.
I give up.
White flag waved.

Caged

Today is hard.
It's the opposite of freedom.
I'm caged. Rabid. Feral.
I want to fight it off—
The day, the week, the year.
I need to escape to a new tomorrow,
And let everything fall into the past.
I want to start brand new,
But I'm choking on everything that already is.
I'm suffocating on what exists.
And there's no way out of that trap.
It's already been sprung, and I'm a captive.
I can dig my nails into the dirt.
I can claw at the walls.
But I know I'll get nowhere.
Life's options have already run dry,
And this is where I ended up.
There are no second or third chances here,
So, I may as well get out of bed...
And face another day in hell.

Firefly Eyes

Your eyes are like summer fireflies.
Lit from somewhere deep within—
A powerful and inexplicable magic.
They flit from place to place,
Taking in the images of the night,
But avoiding my gaze at all costs.
They embrace the darkness,
Safe and protected in its shroud.
Veiled and terrified of the unavoidable dawn.
I know when you allow them to close,
Our time together comes to an end.
You will awaken first, afraid of the light,
And you will run from its glow,
Your escape route visible at dawn.
Your light fades as the sun ignites,
Fearful of any possibility of 'us,'
And you disappear with the coming of the day.
You are my firefly—for nighttime entertainment only.

How Many Times?

How many times can I fade away
Before there's nothing left of myself to hold onto?
Yet again, I rise up and raise my fists to the sky,
Always looking for a fight.
I'll never go down without a struggle,
Without leaving scars in my wake.
But how much of this can I really take
Before I give in, accept defeat, and break?

Are You Happy?

Someone asked me today if I was happy,
And I didn't have an answer.
I mean, I pretend I am.
As the day passed, I thought about it.
An overwhelming sadness took over—
Because no, I'm not happy.
Not even close. Not even a little.
The world spins, days pass, time unravels,
And I watch other people get what they want,
I see them find what they're looking for,
And discover the answers they seek.
People who have caused me the most pain live in bliss.
They've moved on, found love, and left me behind.
I'm still alone—the innocent, left on my own.
No matter how much effort I put in,
I feel like it's never enough.
Never good enough.
Never hard enough.
And I'm over it.
I'll never get where I want to be—

And the fact of the matter is, I'm sick of trying.
I don't want to care anymore. I can't.
I don't want to go through the motions.
I don't want to fake it 'til I make it.
What do I want, then? I don't even know.
All I know is that *this* is not it.
This isn't anything close.
What I'm doing now is so far off from living.
It's merely existing. Surviving but never thriving.
And my problems? All first-world, so bring on the guilt.
I'm blessed. I have more than most.
And, still, I feel like I have nothing.
I feel like I *am* nothing.
I'm not enough. I'll never be enough.
I won't even try anymore.

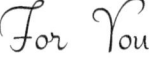

I'm struggling to sparkle in the skies you lay before me.
Lost amidst so many other competing stars,
I'm gasping for the limited air available within your clutches.
But if you asked me to, I'd fall from the skies,
Dive naked into the sea of emptiness that lies beyond,
And lay down my life to become part of the void.
For you, I'd fade into the blackness, the silence,
Becoming both nothing and endless all at the same time.
I'd watch you, veiled in clouds, as you flit amidst the starlight,
Still seeking something from someone else.
Something I would have gladly given.
You could have had all of me, but it was never enough.
I was never the one to illuminate your skies,
Or bring the peace to soothe your darkness.
I was just a distraction. Temporary. Short-term.
To you, I was an easy ending, while I sought a beginning.
I was merely a flicker of light lost to your darkness.
A brief glimmer of hope that faded with the signs of dawn.

Dull

Dull sky, black and blue like a bruise,
Shrouded in cloud cover,
Begging for the sun's glory glow,
To paint it in shades of golden again.

Dull eyes, you left me behind,
Veiled in sin and sorrow,
Aching with the hope of tomorrow,
And the possibility of days to follow.

Dull heart, void of hope,
Covered in bubble wrap and band-aids,
Praying for something more,
A world where you and I exist as one.

Dull voice, nothing left to say,
Parted in silence, lips release no sound,
Dying to reveal all that remains unsaid
About you and me—about us.

But, there is no us to discuss.

Here and Now

You can only hold on for so long,
Bending and yielding under pressure.
It's only a matter of time, mere moments,
Before the weight starts to break you—
Shattering all that was,
Erasing all that came before,
Leaving you with only what little remains.
You can only take what you can carry,
And what's left behind isn't worth having, anyway.
It's a desolate wasteland you find yourself in,
After the fall from where you once stood, so proud.
A far cry from the glitter and gold you once knew.
A distant world, void of the magic you clung to,
Empty of the hope that betrayed you.
You can't hold your head high, anymore,
But at least your heart is protected.
There are no apologies here, no attachments,
Only empty promises and goodbyes.
But, the good news is you won't feel a thing.
There's no magic here; it's forbidden.

No sparks, no glimmers, no future plans.
Here, we've traded possibilities for numbness.
We've offered up love for armor,
And there's no turning back.
This here and now was born of your torment,
And this is all that you will own.

Signs

Dearest red cardinal, are you a sign of loved ones gone?
Do you visit to spread the news that
They're still watching over us?
I've heard that's your role,
But I struggle with the idea of such signs.
I do better with science and proof
Over beliefs that feel blindly accepted.
Just the same, let's talk for a while;
Fill me in on what you've seen.
So, hey there, little bird, how's my mother been?
And, while we're chatting, how are things above?
Have you seen her around lately, can you tell me of her love?
Just a word, a breath, a whisper, something on which to cling,
After she left an earthly battle so cruel and heart-wrenching.
And, succumbing to the force of cancer and death's call,
Red would be a suitable color for her apparel, after all.
The color of a warrior,
A fighter,
A hero,

A woman who held on so long, so strong,
When the odds of survival were near zero.
Little cardinal, tell me you've seen my mother,
Tell her to come by—I need to hear her voice again,
Without it, I can't even find the strength to cry.

Goodbye

I miss the green in your eyes,
The way they sparkled,
And the wrinkles around your smile.
I long to hear your laughter filling the air,
Over things only *we* found funny.
I miss you telling me to wear lipstick,
Even just to leave the house for a minute.
Your memory fades, despite my best efforts
To shelter it, to keep it safe, housed in my heart.
The sound of your voice drifts further away.
Your image is ingrained in me—but now fuzzy.
Safely in my soul, but also somehow less real.
With each passing day—less crisp.
You live on in my heart forever,
But the physical blurs over time,
Stinging more with each passing day.
You are my mother forever and ever,
I just pray I don't ever need a picture to recall
The minute details of your face—
That I don't need a voice recording to recall

The comforting sound of your voice—
The saddest part is that there's no way to
Bring clarity to the fading recollection of your touch.
I will forever miss your hugs, so full of love.
I long to feel your hand in mine,
Holding tight through the darkest night.
… Goodbyes are too hard.

Dating

The sky fades to black once again—
And you walk out the door,
Leaving me breathless and wanting,
Lost amidst the tangled web of:
"I don't know what I want,"
—And—
"I'm not ready for anything serious."
Again and again, we've crossed this bridge,
Only to take ten steps back in the name of:
No labels. No rules. Take it as it comes.
What's wrong with labels, anyway?
What are we now if not a couple?
It's about boundaries and freedom.
But, yours. Only ever yours.
You want yours, but that's where it ends.
You don't want me to have mine,
Knowing damn well I'm tethered to this...
—Whatever *this* is—
Captive like a dog left waiting on a chain,

Starving and cold, wanting something more.
I'm a wanderer, still searching for a home,
Hoping against hope that you'll open your door.
Praying you'll consider the possibility of something more—
But knowing, deep down, that this is a lost cause.

The Rules

Never get too close,
And leave before you get left,
Isn't that how it goes?
Stay one step ahead of the drop.
—The ending, the fall, the shattering—
Get in front of the inevitable tragedy,
Long before it strikes its crushing blow,
And walk where it can't follow.
Always be the one who loves less.
If you love less, they'll hurt more,
And the downward crash may not kill you.
Most importantly, though:
Never let them know how much you care.
Let them think they're a game, and nothing more.
A toy, a plaything, not a piece of your heart—
Then, at least, as far as they know, they can't hurt you.
And—never *ever* let them see you cry.

Gaslit

I'm not sorry for the way it ended.
Far from it, in fact.
My only regret is that it existed at all.
You, with your nonchalant eyes—
Dead inside, they still sparkle,
Pulling me in, your lips rising upward,
Laughing as I hit your cement walls again.
I crash backward against the weight
Of all that you are, only to return again,
Begging, pleading, hoping this time will be different.
How many times can a person come back
Before they finally shatter into a million pieces?
I ask, of course, because you should know by now.
I'm not the first to face your destruction, nor the last.
Not the first to buckle under the weight
Of your inability to love.
No, this certainly isn't your first rodeo, but even so,
Somehow, you'll make it all out to be my fault.
"She was crazy," you'll report to those still listening,

And they'll believe you for your wit and charm.
You'll fool them just the way you did me so many times,
Standing tall as the good guy, strong, proud,
As the truth is shrouded in secrets you will never say aloud.

Toxic

You poison everything you touch,
So, you need a constant supply of new victims.
Unknowing, unprepared, unaware of the true you.
You pull in the next innocent on the list,
Draw them near with venom spewed in secret whispers,
Caresses in the night that you will only take back,
And refuse to acknowledge ever even happened.
You bleed toxic masculinity tainted with insecurity,
And women fall at your feet, trying to "fix" you.
Stand up and fix yourself because, eventually,
They'll see through your sparkling eyes to the lies and alibis.
Your charm comes with an expiration date,
At least, for anyone who can see through your bullshit.
It took a while, but I got there, and so will the others.
And that's why you'll never have anything real—
Because you are straight-up TOXIC,
Unwilling or unable to give yourself to another.
And I've finally realized I've wasted enough time on you.

About the Author

Regina lives with her three children and two rescue dogs in the beautiful Hudson Valley region of New York. She has a B.A. in Environmental Studies and Latin American Studies and a Master's in Public Administration from Pace University.

Before writing and editing full-time, Regina worked as a fundraiser at a global environmental conservation organization and spent several years as a stay-at-home mom. She loves the outdoors, animals, cooking, coffee, and spending her free time with her kids and pets.

Email: ReginaWrites@gmail.com
www.ReginaBergen.com

Also by Regina Bergen

Small Town Dirt Series

Dirty Hoe: A Gardening Romance (Small Town Dirt Book 1)

Dirty Latte: A Coffee Shop Romance (Small Town Dirt Book 2)

www.ingramcontent.com/pod-product-compliance
Lightning Source LLC
LaVergne TN
LVHW041229080426
835508LV00011B/1124